And the Word became flesh and lived among us.

John 1:14

PORTRAITS OF GRACE

PORTRAITS OF GRACE

Images and Words from the Monastery of the Holy Spirit

James Stephen Behrens, OCSO

Foreword by Patrick Hart, OCSO

acta
PUBLICATIONS

PORTRAITS OF GRACE
Images and Words from the Monastery of the Holy Spirit
by James Stephen Behrens, OCSO
with a Foreword by Patrick Hart, OCSO

Edited by L.C. Fiore
Cover Design by Tom A. Wright
Text design and typesetting by Patricia A. Lynch
Author photo credit: Chaminade Crabtree, OCSO

Scripture quotations are from the *New Revised Standard Version Bible*, copyright 1989 by the Division of Christian Education of the National Council of the Churches of Christ in the USA. Used by permission.

Published by ACTA Publications, 5559 W. Howard St., Skokie, IL 60077
(800) 397-2282, www.actapublications.com

Library of Congress Control Number: 2007927590
ISBN: 978-0-87946-334-2
Printed in Korea by Graphics TwoFortyFour, Inc
Year: 13 12 11 10 09 08 07
Printing: 10 9 8 7 6 5 4 3 2 1

Foreword

In *Portraits of Grace*, James Stephen Behrens combines brief texts of singular depth and his own extraordinarily beautiful photographs. With this volume, he completes a trilogy of books examining grace in the prosaic of daily life. Although he focuses his lens on the ordinary, he captures something of the divine design in all of Creation, especially in the most mundane details.

Behrens, like so much of Thomas Merton, uses his camera as a contemplative instrument as he casually makes his way around the Monastery of the Holy Spirit in Conyers, Georgia. His images and corresponding words draw the viewer into a profound silence, wondering at the beauty of God's creation in the lowly and hidden aspects of life. As a result, God shines through all of creation, even while this volume focuses on the seemingly commonplace. As a great minimalist poet put it succinctly: "Less is more."

Father Behrens was a diocesan priest for twenty years in Newark, New Jersey, before entering the Monastery of the Holy Spirit. His post-graduate work on the writings of the southern novelist, Walker Percy, is evident in all of his prose. He has just been appointed Guest Master at the Monastery of the Holy Spirit and spends his time nurturing the retreatants as well as the bonsai plants.

I first discovered Behrens' writings as short pieces that appeared in a syndicated column in the *National Catholic Reporter*, and was deeply impressed by his simple style. He always made me pause and contemplate the truths hidden beneath his lean prose. Soon after the publication of his first volume in the trilogy, *Grace is Everywhere: Reflections of an Aspiring Monk*, I felt compelled to review it for a small monastic newsletter, since I wanted to alert the monastic world to this new and deceptively simple Cistercian author.

Shortly after this, I had the privilege of meeting Father James at the Monastery of Holy Spirit while attending the abbatial blessing of their previous abbot. I was delighted to find him to be a very warm and welcoming monk, no different from the writer who wrote so disarmingly on grace in the ordinary experiences of life. For James Stephen Behrens (and as it should be for everyone), all is grace, all is pure gift.

Patrick Hart, OCSO
17 May 2007
+ Feast of the Ascension

For Mae and Jane

with love and gratitude

Candle Holder on Wall

We live in the light that is God,
and yet we wait for it.

Beauty Right Outside Your Window

We live with the myth of the Eternal Upgrade. Better things, better people, better advantages—almost a better anything lies just ahead. All we need to do is acquire whatever it is we need. There always seems to be something just ahead of us, changing shape with each change of fortune. It can be exhausting, trying to seize what we never can have.

But we can be captivated by something else: the allure of the here and now.

It requires a different kind of energy to take a good and loving look at what is close at hand. Many poems invite us to savor what is nearer to us—the charm of ordinary days, ordinary roads or ordinary people. That which is extraordinary in life is close to each of us in abundance.

Age and Beauty

Years add a wondrous beauty to life. Age ripens with each passing season. The light of God shines in a special way through what is old and beautiful.

Like the Sky

We do not adapt well to change. Routine is important to us and it is difficult to deal with sudden or even slow changes. It would be easier if we could learn to embrace change in all its forms.

Our lives are like the sky. Things are not the same from one minute to the next, even though we enjoy relative periods of stability.

People and events are moving through our lives all the time. And we all know sunny days and cloudy days in terms of our moods and dispositions. Most people find the sky beautiful—most people love the change of clouds, colors and variations in the weather. Maybe our love for the sky can help us be more patient with our own changes from one horizon, one day, to another.

Slow Rides

A crisis mounts over the price of gasoline. As the cost per gallon increases, perhaps people will take to a different set of wheels and get to where they need to go in a way that is healthier and allows some time for calm thinking… for sightseeing.

Green Bottle and Lighted Shed Window

We pass by familiar things and familiar faces every day of our lives. They may become so familiar that we do not see them—really see them—anymore. It can take a shift of perspective to see them in a different light. It can be the most ordinary thing or the most taken-for-granted person, but with a bit of reflection beauty can emerge.

The sources for inspiration are many, and they are readily available. All it takes is a bit of time to open our eyes to what is beneath our feet, through a window, or in the life of someone whose tender heart contains a story waiting to be told.

Jesus saw remarkable things all around him. Seeds, the wind, the poor, the rich, fig trees and the sea—he used these to explain the wonders of God. We journey through treasures every day of our lives. They are not ours to possess; they are on loan so that we might learn to trust and love the Lender. ⬭

We journey through treasures every day of our lives.

Church Psalters

The writer Joan Didion suffered enormous loss in the span of one year. Her husband died, followed one year later by their only daughter. Didion has said that she writes to give clarity to her experience—so much so that she does not quite know what something means until she labors to put it into words. And indeed, her prose affords us a clear glimpse of the world as she sees it.

Religious texts, specifically the Psalms, offer a window to the history of a people and their God. There too a people struggle to come to terms with loss, over and over again. All the joys and sorrows of life find expression in the Psalms, and the words of the Psalms have brought comfort to people of all ages and in all ages.

Trust

Each step entails trust. We may not think about it all that much as we walk through any given day, but we surely think about it if our sight or hearing fails or if we find ourselves in a dark place. Then we realize we have to trust in whatever light we have to help us along.

At its best, spirituality opens us to ways of trusting in the darkest times. When our senses fail and we feel lost, we are most vulnerable to the God who comes to us through the kindness of others—and it is then we know what kind of a light we human beings can be.

Slow Beauty

I read of a poet who took years to write a few lines of poetry. She would return again and again to these lines, honing them, crafting them until the words held depth and vision. Writing that way was a real labor.

To look at those few lines, you would not think it could have taken such a long time to write them. But maybe what is deepest in us can only be expressed in a few words. If they are words of love, longing and hope, it may take a while to move deeply enough into our heart to find them.

Poetry was her way of finding God, the Living Word that rests in each of us.

Poetry was her way of finding God, the Living Word that rests in each of us.

Light and Shovel

We cannot absorb the love of God all at once. Perhaps that is why in many Old Testament passages there are cautionary procedures taken when a person is approached by the Divine. Just a glimpse is allowed, and at times not even that. All Moses saw was the glow of a fire. The gift and warmth of that light concealed the appearance of God.

Maybe God is shy. Or extremely powerful, radiating something we cannot absorb all at once. Maybe God comes, bit by bit, into a world always in need of holy light.

When the light came into the world we all became bearers of the light through the Spirit. So why do we find words of love difficult to express? The language of love is the light within us; it does not come readily in ordinary conversation. Perhaps, like God, we can speak it only a little bit at a time. Perhaps we are more God-like than we know.

Low Incoming Housing

Some of the best high-rises are close to the earth.

27

Getting Things Right

There are days when nothing seems to go right. We spill our morning coffee; our car won't start; we miss our subway or bus and walk absent-mindedly through a puddle. There are no ways to avoid days like this, much less predict them, and there aren't any ways to make things always go right.

Nothing in life is perfect.

So we muster our patience and just let those days be. But on our good days, we can try to be sensitive to those whose days are upside down. Each and every day we will surely run into someone whose daily cart has flipped—a little kindness can go a long way. When you see friends whose wheels are pointing skyward, do the best you can to help them.

The Path of Life

We look down at our feet and move them a little bit. We are on some sort of path. We walk forward and the path guides us to where we want to go.

Christianity was, in the early centuries, known as the Way: The way to God was through the experience of loving. Jesus is synonymous with the Way because he is the "Way, the truth and the light" (John 14:6). When we love, we walk his walk, talk his talk, and become something of him along his road.

So as we walk, we keep our head up, our heart open, and our eyes bright with expectation. The light moves and is always just ahead. Ahead of all of us, guiding us with hope and warmth.

Morning

How beautiful is the morning.

The Brighter the Light

The brighter the light, the more we see.

A New Day

Worries have a way of accumulating during the day so that by the time evening falls, their weight is burdensome. And so, evenings are probably not the best time to make any significant decisions.

A good night's rest and the freshness of morning can make a lot of difference in the way we see things. Life is a lighter affair, come morning.

Wisdom is not to be had from worrying late into the night. It comes as we sleep and remains with us through the dawn.

Much of Life Is Waiting

We all seem to be waiting for someone or something.

Spreading the News

We hear things in all sorts of ways: word of mouth, radio and television, telephones and cell phones. Leaflets cover windshields and there is graffiti on the walls of every city on earth. We seem to have a need to spread news fast, and there are always more upgrades, improvements or abilities to enhance.

Life travels in fascinating ways. Seeds fly at the mercy of the wind, spores come through open windows, tiny creatures seek each other out in the coldest and hottest places imaginable. God was certainly inventive in the way life proliferates.

The Word is life. It desires to live, to inhabit new places and new hearts. It rides on the winds of love and hope and needs no special language or culture to find a home. It settles and grows wherever there are people of good will. It thrives in all seasons, rides winds high and low, delights in the random and seemingly impossible. It lives because it is God's news, God's life, God's way of speaking.

The Word is life.... It thrives in all seasons,
rides winds high and low, delights in the random and seemingly impossible.

New Words, New Day

It may be words on a page or words from a friend.
It may be the Word that is spoken by God.
Words invite us to what is new, hopeful, promising.

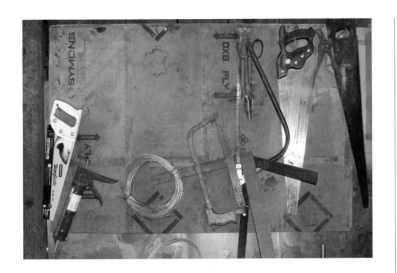

Labor

Genesis does not give any indication that God created time.

We must assume that God took a sliver of the eternal and stretched it just a little bit. Exactly how God did that we don't know, but we do know that time altered everything—granting a past, present and future (and all the nuanced, grammar-school variations we learned) to everything.

And so it is that we labor with language to situate ourselves within all that we see and do. There is little we can do about time, other than trust with our hearts that our labor is sharing in God's plan to one day make life perfect and beautiful.

Retirement Home

When our wheels slow and we are tired.

Truth

Everything speaks a kind of truth.

Blue Stormy Barn

Fear cripples us. A mild case of fear robs us of the ability to speak and freezes our natural response. A severe case of fear drives us to behavior that is best described as panic.

Even little fears can cast a pall over our hearts.

It is good to talk these fears over with a trusted friend. After all, he or she has probably "been there" too. The fear soon passes and things brighten up. A friendship is deepened because we trusted someone.

The Airplane

There was a monk who wanted as primitive a life as possible. He chose to live in the mountains, far from the distractions of modern life: the noise, the rapid pace, the interruptions.

He was not there too long before the noise of jets passing high overhead began to bother him. And it was not long after that he returned to the monastery, booked a flight to an even more remote area, and flew there.

Perhaps he found some peace and quiet in economy class.

Each Person Is a Revelation

To best understand the differences between one thing or another, concentrate on what they have in common. This is also the practice of taxonomists—men and women who spend lifetimes classifying the billions of things that fill the world, trying to provide order and cohesion to the dizzying variations that exist within and among species. There are also those who study humanity with the hope of discerning God, the Creator.

Is there any one thing that all people have in common that can be called a universally-shared trait? We are all born and we all die. We know pain and we know joy. But these are attributes of most living things.

When it comes to being human, things get more complicated. Moral values, methods of knowledge and ways of loving vary from person to person and culture to culture. We can, however, learn to view one another as windows through which God's wondrous goods can be seen: That is one of the finer modes of window shopping.

To best understand the differences between one thing or another,
concentrate on what they have in common.

Signatures

We like to let people know that we were here, that we passed through this life and left some kind of a mark. We celebrate our milestones.

There are carvings on trees. There is graffiti on walls. There are pyramids and great monuments. They all seek to convey a name, an accomplishment, a sign that someone was here and did something.

God leaves signatures every second of every day. God's writing is on every face, in every walk of life. The signature of God reveals itself when we learn to see life simply and lovingly. If we respond to the invitation, we learn to write like God. And that is a lasting and beautiful mark to leave behind.

Angel in Shed

We live in a world where spirit and matter interplay and interweave. Our labor is no small effort as we wrestle spirit from its latent presence in the world. The tools of our hands, hearts and minds can make great strides in revealing the spirit as it gives way to our desire to create beauty, to speak truth, to adorn life.

Adam and Eve were banished from Eden, a place of eternal beauty in all its forms. But God enabled them to redeem themselves—and the world—through labor. God sent the Spirit to ensure that labor is not a fruitless toil. We partake in the world of Spirit whenever we labor with love.

In the Details

It is only by using a camera fearlessly and repeatedly that we learn its nuances. For example, the aperture allows light to enter through the lens. A narrow aperture gives much finer detail but requires a longer shutter speed, while a wide aperture provides less depth of field and sacrifices some detail (and requires a more rapid shutter speed). A narrow aperture requires that the camera be held very still. It takes longer for the light to make its imprint on the film or digital card.

The heart can also take in much with a seemingly narrow adjustment to life's scenery.

We can love very well without moving much at all. A lot of detail can be absorbed into our heart through a careful focusing on what is at hand. It may take longer to learn to see the great through the small. Why rush through life and miss most of the scenery?

God the Potter

Long ago, a human looked at his or her hand and realized the hand could hold. Voila: the first pot.

Leaves hold water; gravity holds the earth and waves; orbits hold their planets; parents hold children; cups hold coffee; shelves hold everything and anything; a picture holds a thousand words and a thousand words can hold a dream. A heart contains, a mind grasps, breaths are held and seats and sofas retain.

God holds us so that we might learn what it means to hold each other. Voila: God fashions us as a potter so that we might hold divine love.

Simple Things

There are no advertisements that encourage us to buy less, resist shopping, or use what we presently have. The only upgrade that comes with goodness is consistency. The one improvement that comes with kindness is sincerity. Many good things come in small, long-lasting packages—not the least of which is the human heart.

It becomes better with use. It can even work, just as before, when totally replaced by plastic. It is very easy to clean—a bit of truth every day with someone we love. The only way we can lose it is by giving it away; but in that wondrous process it comes back to us four-fold.

The smallest things seem to go the farthest when they need to accomplish something big.

Obstacles

We are raised to pretend our lives are success stories in the making. The more obstacles we overcome, the more successful we are. But failure has a troubling place in the scenario—we don't know what to do with it.

To the extent we find it difficult to accept our own inevitable failures, we cannot accept the failures of others. But what really makes a successful life? We are frail beings and life is a delicate affair. To accept failure is not to say that we didn't try to do well. Rather, it is a sober realization that there are obstacles that we will surely fail to overcome.

But we can learn something very important from our failures.

Growth emerges in ways we cannot predict or control. There may be a situation so hardened with difficulties that we simply have to endure it, to get through it as best we can. Accepting failure softens our heart and endows us with a sensitivity that we never would have had if we didn't hang in there and learn from our trials. It's amazing what we can grow through—like a vine growing right through a wall.

Forgiveness

Imagine if the seasons held grudges. Autumn would delay winter. Winter would kill spring. Spring might stall summer. Summer might let autumn wait. But as it is, seasons have no memory of the good and bad that accompany them. One season passes and gives way to the next.

We have our own seasons and they can be seasons of joy or sorrow. Happiness may come like warmth from the sun. Bitterness may pelt us like rain.

There is an art to learning from the wisdom of nature. While we can't control most of what comes our way, we can learn to accept it with grace. We can learn to let go of what hurts and forgive those who hurt us. There can be no life without seasons, and there can be no life of the heart without learning to rise in love and turn toward indifference with courage. We adapt to each season—be still and learn from the sun, the cold, the wind and rain, the snow and seeds.

Paint Colors

The heart expresses itself in many ways. It can see, feel, hear, know. Joy and sorrow reside in the heart and these find a way to speak.

The language of the heart speaks in many ways. Its voice can rest on canvas, be spoken with the tongue or conveyed through a touch. Finding our heart's voice can take a while. But patience and discipline eventually pay off.

The world is an array of language, most of it silent, which reveals the depth and contours of the human heart.

God the Artist

With time, love and care we can create things of beauty.
God does the same with us, stroke by stroke.

A Place Apart

We all need a place to nurture our inner selves, an intimate spot we find conducive to reading, writing, or just "being" for a while—a place we can settle down and feel at home. Self-knowledge comes when we take the time to listen to our hearts and really hear what is going on in our place of need, love, forgiveness and hope.

Such places are as varied as they are available. For some, it is a walk on a beach; others may find peace on a bench in a park. For a young girl in Manhattan, her special get-away place is a fire escape that affords a view of the city lights, the people and the cars passing below. She dreams of the good things she may become when she grows up.

Our place apart is near us. It calls to us. Let's follow its call and be at peace, if only for a little while.

Bad Hair Day

We all have our bad hair days.

Patience

We want something and we want it right away. Our mind goes into overdrive, trying to find ways to make it happen, make it arrive, make it right. In our need to have it, other things lose their appeal or lose our attention.

All of us have needs, but we have become so used to their immediate fulfillment that we tend to forget the most important things in life. Indeed, we forget life itself.

God gave us patience so that we might learn what is really good for us. Waiting is the very essence of how life became the beautiful mystery that it is. Creation is yet in the making—and so are we.

Different Ways to God

Literature, in all its wondrous variety, opens a reader to many worlds. It is a fine way to travel. The pleasure of the text lies precisely in its ability to carry people to places that require no more movement than the leisurely turn of a page and the delicate focusing of the eye. We read, and we go.

God spoke a word. And that Word is life, the life that is God's son.

Yet Jesus did not leave behind a text. We know that he could write but apparently he was not interested in writing things down.

We are his text, his living words. If he best spoke by teaching us how to love, there is no better language to learn. The grammar of God is known through loving and being loved. In this sense, God's language is the only universal language that is known to men and women all over the world.

Church Columns

Each day has a vast array of beauty. Take the time to notice it.

It is an interesting habit to develop. The more we give ourselves time to see it, the more beauty will reveal itself to us.

It is a very generous mystery.

Spider Webs

Tiny creatures use intricate designs to catch what they need in order to live.

Is it love God spins all around us, to bring us nearer?

Born Anew

Life, in all its forms, emerges into being after a period of gestation. There are wombs and nests, seeds and eggs and husks: places of preparation where new life waits. All around us, every second of our lives, countless mysteries entwine. The orchestrations of timing and temperature, light and darkness, nurture and movement—these interplay with each other in a delicate, finely-tuned, cooperative arrangement.

The arrangement is a living and ongoing drama from which life emerges.

We live our years in the universal womb of God's design. We embrace this waiting in faith. In and through God's time, all is now being born anew.

Soft and Hard Things

Each of us knows what it's like to experience hardness of heart. There are times when we find it very difficult to apologize, or to forgive, or to let our defenses down.

When we feel stubbornness eating at us, a prayer can help too.

Simply put, we are not happy when we are resentful or unforgiving. We are happiest when we are free from whatever keeps our heart from loving.

Window Opening to Windows

A librarian was recently cleaning out an old cabinet in an even-older library. At the bottom of one drawer was a pile of papers, all aged and apparently not of much worth. At the bottom of the pile she saw one page of a musical score. She lifted the manuscript, examined it, and turned over the page to find more notations. It was a long-lost composition of Beethoven's, written in his own hand. A rare find, indeed. A treasure at the bottom of the heap. A treasure that many lovers of classical music would deem priceless.

There are many things waiting to be opened. There are doors and windows, hearts and minds, the slow unfolding of the day. Old things will be found, faded loves will be renewed, hurting hearts will be given hope.

God hides treasures everywhere. We need the courage to open what we leave closed. There are treasures to be had. One way opens for us: not darkness but light, and more openings in the distance.

Cross on Slab

We set things aside to mark significance. Days on calendars are highlighted for happy and sad occasions. Precious objects adorn a table or are placed under glass. This goes back to pre-historic times—which are in themselves something of a contradiction. Apparently the peoples of pre-history were aware that objects had a special place—be they simple beads or etchings on a cave wall.

All things in heaven and earth have been set aside by God, a providential plan for transformation.

All that we know and all that we are comes from God, for God "saw everything that he had made, and indeed, it was very good" (Genesis 1:31). The universe is sacred prior to whatever religious aspirations we may entertain about it. It is good—signed with a love that comes from God.

New Foundations

Even the best foundations eventually corrode. They give way to the ravages of time. The gift of faith is said to be a sure foundation, one that can endure the worst assaults of time, age and wear.

Yet faith, in its best expression, is a gift to support others. Inevitably, everything around us will crumble and fall. With all the strength that we can muster we can lend a hand to help someone who has fallen. When our time comes, when weakness lays claim to the foundations of our lives, others of strong faith will hopefully and lovingly hold us in our weakness.

The Hidden God

Words can be like a finely-woven net in which we hope to snare God.
Perhaps God has nets as well. Many of them.

Letters

The man wrote an essay. He wrote of being sad because his wife had passed on. His heartache deepened because he wished she had written to him while she was alive.

Their marriage was good and they shared deeply and lovingly all through their years together. But they were never far apart enough to correspond by letter.

I would tell him to be still, to hold close to his heart the memories. His heart is where she wrote clearly and deeply with the most lasting and beautiful ink there is.

Road Side Wisdom

Some words add years to our life.

Treasure in Field

Jesus said the Kingdom is like a treasure hidden in a field (see Matthew 13:44). Happiness or peace, security or God—indeed any or all of these—are much closer than we think. It might be a risk to let go of our more fanciful treasure hunts and start looking at the more intimate and proximate places of our lives.

God is not a God of a better tomorrow or a newly discovered way of life that might be found through looking far and wide. God is near, in the very soil of our lives.

Words and Silence

There is a page in our monastic Antiphonary that concludes the end of one of the liturgical seasons. The page has four words written on it: " This page is blank." The other pages, of course, do not say, "This page has words."

Maybe the monk who put those words there did not trust the intelligence of the other monks. I am sure he was well-intentioned, but apparently he did not trust how obvious the blank page was—he wanted to give directions. Or maybe a blank page really bothered him; he had to put something there.

We should try to resist the urge to put words where no words are necessary. We share God's life and so we share with him the language and the wisdom of the unspoken. Jesus asks that we trust the Spirit to speak through us—we don't need to worry about words.

Open Windows

We know enough to open windows and let in fresh air.
The heart needs to breathe as well—it needs to be opened.

The Happy Buddhas

Friendship divides our grief and doubles our joy. Our covenant with God is one of friendship. But there is no friend who can remove our sorrows. Nor can we do that for any friend of ours. But we have friends who are a joy to know, and we hope there are those who find some joy in knowing us.

Friendship is a great and rare gift. We try to remember not to take our friends for granted; we do our best to tell them how much they mean to us. They have made all the difference in our lives. So much of what we know of God we know through the gift of friendship.

It is good to walk this life with friends. Memories stored and shared, rough times made smoother, our load lightened by happy times. Throughout it all, God is there, giving to us through friendship. And so I thank God for being quite close—as close as a hug, a phone call, a shared meal.

The Light at One's Feet

When it is dark, we walk carefully, our eyes focused on our feet, hoping for some sure sense with which to find our way. It helps to walk alongside someone else when it is dark, for the sense of direction that he or she may offer. Even a far light in the distance will not illuminate a night path, but another person can be a big help if they are more gifted with "night vision."

God's light is just like that. Always present, right at our feet, freeing us to move ahead without fear of getting lost. God is, to quote the psalmist, "a lamp to our feet and a light to our path" (Psalm 119:105). Those words were chanted in a time when light was hard to come by, especially at night.

As a people, the church is light. We gather together so that we might be light to each other. And when we walk through life, we do so with the light ahead and right at our feet—a light that draws us forward, out of the night, lighting each and every step of the way.

A Sense of Home

Everyone needs a place to call home, a place to feel secure. For the vast majority of us, homemaking comes quite naturally. Still, there are others who have no place to call home. Millions go homeless every day, and much of this tragedy is caused by human cruelty.

Instead of churches spending money on their own self-preservation, they could tighten their belts and send contributions to charitable organizations that provide food and shelter for the desperate of this world. It is how we make this world a better home for everyone.

God gave the simplest of animals the means to provide shelter for themselves. God gave us a talent as well—to give from our surplus to help those in need.

Dove on Fountain

The stage manager in Thornton Wilder's play *Our Town* says, at one point in the play, "There is something eternal to things." That "something eternal" lives in us, but we need time apart to better see it and learn from it.

The world can be a much kinder place when seen in light of its eternal dimension.

All that we love is of and in God. Faith is a way of finding life. We all need a place to collect—to gather within us all that we are before we take wing once again into one another's lives.

Page of Writing

A poet sent me a book of his poetry. He wrote poem after poem about the need for love in a world torn by violence, war and other hatreds. The poet said that writing poems was a way for him to find his heart, to better see that which was real in the world. His voice was admittedly small—the book had a very modest circulation and he was not well-known in the world of poetry.

I have never met this man, but in the letters we have exchanged I feel I have been given the gift of friend-ship with a great and towering human being. His words bear the marks of a deeply human heart.

I am glad that he writes. His words give me reason to embrace the power, the telling beauty, of the seem-ingly small and insignificant. Some day, his labors will bear real fruit—the best of our words are harbingers of a life to come.

Stone Slabs on Mud

We have many institutional programs that offer career plans. These plans are enshrined in diplomas, certificates, licenses and degrees galore. With any one of these, or a combination, we have the means to succeed on a chosen path. Yet once we embark, it is not too long before we realize how troublesome a road it is, for it is a road paved by human lives.

Kindness is one stepping stone. Patience, another. Faith links these stepping stones together into a path so we can find our way through life. We may find a few spots that need a stone or two. We should lay down a bit of hope, a sign of love, or an act of faith to make the road easier for someone behind us who needs some sure-footedness.

As the years pass, those things we hang on our walls may fade. But if we have done our best to lay goodness where we found it lacking, the brief time we spent will have paid off. A life well-lived for others is as good as any program gets.

Mike's Tools

Life is an ongoing series of adjustments, adaptations, refinements. Any maturing relationship involves a need to fine-tune the heart to love. Love may never ask the same thing twice—it is that generous in its reach and expectation.

If we were made to love and to be loved, and if life reveals itself through the way we learn to love it, part of being open to this gift is learning to trust the Designer. The Spirit is God's creative tool, turning all that exists toward a more loving, fuller life.

Tree Climbing

Kids love to climb trees. The bigger the tree, the better. We loved climbing trees once, but we cannot remember the last tree we climbed. A day came when we climbed the last tree and that was that.

Maybe tree-climbing morphs into something else. Enticing limbs, branches and the sought-for heights give way to other adventures.

Bookstores boast a lot of aisles; love has many avenues. Labor offers creative heights to climb; prayer invites us to branch out in the ways of the Spirit. A new day offers a new approach to life's problems, and mysteries can be glimpsed when we pause to ponder the beauty of all that we can see.

Empty Bowl Theology

We ask God for many things. We approach God to fill our lives with meaning, with hope, with a sense of presence in a world that so desperately needs a sign of the divine.

What if God has been coming all the time through that which needs to be filled? What if God is an empty stomach, a broken heart, an anguished cry, an empty bowl?

We have a tendency to want to heal and fill and satisfy. Maybe God has come closer than we think. Everything that is empty has left room for God to arrive, again and again.

Human Potential

Human potential is delicate. It relies on many external sources, the most important being the love and encouragement of others.

There are periods of discouragement when we feel the chill of weathering yet another muted dream or thwarted try. At our worst, we may feel like our energies are so depleted we will never get moving again. But then a warm smile or the supportive words of another can bring us to a place where we can once again experience life in a positive way.

The continued growth of becoming the person God calls us to be: That call comes through those who love us and beckons us to be people who contribute to life by giving from our hearts. After all, hearts take time to grow too.

Seasons and Life

Seasons come and go, within us and about us, bringing ever more life and beauty.

Pecan Shells

We emerge from a dizzying array of people, places, events, circumstances—these help create who we are and where we come from. As Christians we believe that all of life emerges from God, long ago and at this very second. God created life and also sustains it. It is impossible to take in the whole picture, to trace all the threads of the tapestry that stretch back in time and of which we are a living part. So maybe it is wise to think small, to ponder how we were given life, sheltered by family and then, hopefully, grew into a maturity that allowed us to branch out on our own.

There are those who we care for with love. There are those who depend on us for shelter, warmth and a sense of meaning or goodness. These are enormous gifts for which we should be grateful. We have been blessed with something that has been in the works a long, long time.

The best "thank you" is to do the best we can for those who are coming after us, those who are in our care and deserve a better world. After all, that is what we were given by those who nurtured us.

Twisting Twigs

No one sings a song in exactly the same way,
and no one realizes his or her potential in the same way.

There are gifts that come to people quite naturally and with apparent ease. Others intuit a gift and labor long and hard to bring it to expression. Prodigies may compose a symphony in their youth, but there are late-bloomers who will not reach their artistic peaks until much later in life.

Yet it is the gift that matters—the time involved doesn't matter at all. There are writers whose fits and starts over the years were an inevitable part of the creative process. But this was not revealed to them until much later. Only at the emergence of the finished work does the writer see the struggle as a necessary part of the birthing.

God made us differently. We may look about and envy those for whom a song comes readily and for those whose voice comes easily. But the music of God has a lot of varied notes and tempos. No one sings a song in exactly the same way, and no one realizes his or her potential in the same way. What beauty those differences are!

Knock and It Will Be Opened

It is easy to knock on a lot of wrong doors. But we keep knocking, hoping that someone will open up and let us into the roomy corridors of life's purpose.

Knock on the door of a happy person. He or she will hear the knock and be glad to share their space—and in doing so, teach us how to find our own space, our own meaning, our own happiness.

Stress

Stress leads to many things: frayed nerves, high blood pressure, restless nights. Maybe one way to ease our stress is to find something we love to do. If there are knots around our heart, there are ways to loosen them a bit.

We need to find something for which we have a passion. It may be writing or taking walks, photography or art, reading or knitting. A little physical activity helps.

Doing something that promotes a high level of satisfaction offsets stress. Tension is caused by the more problematic aspects of human living. Warm feelings going in the right direction can relax our whole being.

And if we can't find that special something, we should try not to lose sleep over it. Maybe we can develop a passion for the very act of searching for that special someone or something to bring out the best in us.

Aging

We grow old and broken. The contents of our lives spill over the years and into the years. Aging seems like a process that happens only to others, but as we live day by day, moments of love, goodness and kindness are like seeds in the lives of others.

We were born to live so that others may take from our lives.

Where there is growth, nothing is lost. And perhaps the purest love comes in our later years when we can love with wisdom, patience and gratitude for what the years have taught us—for those who spilled their lives into us.

Gas Meter

We live in a society that offers a comprehensive array of things designed to improve our lives. All of it is constantly upgraded, more often than not for a fee—health programs multiply; self-help books fill every bookstore; spiritualities vie for one another and more are imported or dreamed up every day.

We consume whatever we can afford in order to enhance our lives. But with all of this, we can feel empty. There is that pesky little something in us that resists complete satisfaction. Saint Augustine called it the "restlessness" that will not know rest until it rests in God.

That emptiness is a special place nothing can fill, save God. If left alone, there can be found a peace that is more accepting of human limitation, human folly. We can either ride through life on a near-empty tank and never worry about filling up, or we can be aware of our emptiness and learn from it, draw peace from it, let it be.

Largeness of Heart

The pupil of an eye is small, but it can see the expanse of a city skyline. It can take in the vast stretches of the universe.

The human heart is a bit larger and it too has a way of seeing. The sight of a crowd can excite the eyes with many things; it can also move the heart to a place of love, compassion and hope.

There are things we can do to refine sight. We can wear glasses, squint, or take a closer look. And there are things we can and should do to hone what the heart sees. We can pray, meditate, be still. The way we learn to see makes all the difference in our perspective: whether we see abundance or we see scarcity.

Cloister Columns

We seek words to express our joys and sorrows. Life is interplay between these two experiences and we hope we come to know more joy than sorrow.

Many an ancient myth offers reasons for the co-existence of light and darkness. Genesis tells us that God separated light from darkness and found that it was good (see Genesis 1:4). Joy brings us light. Sorrow darkens our souls.

Friendship enables us to share our joys and divide our sorrows. Many a church edifice magnificently arranges the windows and walls so that the light and shadow co-exist and complement one another. The blend of light and shadow enhances the beauty of these places of worship. We can learn from what we build to better walk through life, carrying the light and darkness of our hearts.

Thirsty Boots

Eric Andersen has a song called "Thirsty Boots." Who knows what the song is about—do boots really thirst? Maybe our feet can thirst for the road if the place we need to go is important enough.

Some people get their boots wet and leave them on a window sill. It is hard to tell, sometimes, why people do the things they do. But the song says that boots get thirsty.

We do funny things, things that may seem strange at first. But a song can be written about us and beauty can be made from the things we do. It is a nice way to walk through life, taking what may seem strange and giving it a place of beauty in a song. We all thirst for something good. The walk is worth getting our feet wet.

Troubles

Life often presents problematic situations. Our first instinct may be to remedy the dilemma by relying on personal resources. But it may be better to rely on the kindness of others.

Leaf on a Thread

Life reveals beauty to the extent we risk loving it.

Life is as brief as it is delicate. We are more vulnerable than we care to admit; we live suspended between birth and death. We came from God and we will return to God, but this "in-between time" requires no small amount of courage to understand the meaning of what we have been given.

The life of Jesus was fragile. He was vulnerable—he allowed his heart to be open and read by a lot of people. If the meaning of life can be taken from his heart, it would reveal that love is what keeps all beautiful things suspended in grace.

God holds all things, from the vast cosmos to the tiniest creatures, in the palm of his hand. Faith is the way of trusting in the God who holds us. He brought us into life and will one day call us home. Until that day, life is to be lived by holding on to it. Life reveals beauty to the extent we risk loving it.

Friends

It is a great blessing to have a friend. A friend is someone to lean on, someone with whom we share joys and sorrows, someone with whom silence can be shared comfortably.

God seeks to befriend us and share our lives with us. Friendship with God can grow to the point where we can find long periods of silence comforting.

God speaks through silence: the silence of beauty and the silence of simple things.

Little Wooden Pig

One of the monks told me he had had a rough few days. I saw him taking a walk around the monastery and he looked as if he had lost his way. He would stop every ten feet or so and look around, appear to get his bearings, and then move on—only to stop again. He looked as if he did not know where to go or what to do. But he kept walking. He is certainly familiar with the terrain; he has lived here for over thirty years. When I asked him later, he said it was just "one of those days." It was, he said, as if he were lost and could not find his way back to the familiar routine of feeling at home. He then said he was glad I cared enough to ask and that he felt better already. A kind word can give welcome direction to the temporarily disoriented.

I can understand. Such a strange sense envelopes me every now and then. These are, I know, not good times to make decisions or to try and settle something that might require steady thinking. Perhaps it is best to walk, as my friend did, and look around.

Sometimes life is exhilarating, other times life overwhelms, while some days life is just a matter of groping through the unfamiliar…and even around the familiar.

A kind word can give welcome direction to the temporarily disoriented.

The Road Is Narrow

Jesus said the road to Life is narrow and rough and that few people find it (see Matthew 7:14). May those who do find Life show the rest of us errant pilgrims the way.

Closed Bonsai Window

We sometimes shy away from a compliment. Something in us shuts down when we are the focus of attention. It is the rare person who learns to accept praise gracefully and with an open and joyous heart.

The light that is the love of others shines all around us. In time, if we learn to trust it, it will open us to what it wants to reveal.

Every day we see what light accomplishes for so many living things. We need to become more like the Light from whence we came, the Light that is always within loving distance. It is, as the saying goes, right outside our window.

Books on Shelf

Words, carefully written, reveal worlds near and far.
Love, freely given, reveals the only world there really is.

Light on Scriptorium Wall

We walk through a room in late afternoon and are suddenly struck by how lovely the light is as it falls across walls and through windows. The light is there on most days, whether we pass through the room or not. Night comes, or the rains come, and the light recedes, only to come again on another late, beautiful afternoon.

Praying Mantis

The psalmist writes that life is but "a breath…a passing shadow" (Psalm 144:4). But so much beauty is given in that brevity—in the smallest glimpses of life. The scene of a patch of blue on which a delicate and tiny creature walks carefully amidst dew-drops gives me reason to pause and ponder the gift of the eternal that walks gently on a morning glory.

Day Lessons

Seasons come and go, but in their passing they never fail to sow the seeds of renewal. Life is high—and low—tides.

Colored Brick Wall

When we hit the proverbial brick wall and find there is no way around it or even through it, the best we can do is take a good look at the situation and say a prayer for something good to come from it.

If we are patient, some shade of meaning will emerge— even a bit of color.

Words and Light

It is wondrous to watch a baby's eyes as he or she begins to recognize light as an object. The beauty of light elicits a delighted smile. It is probably one of the first wonders of the child's world, bringing such awe to one so little.

We are attracted to light throughout our lives. If love, intelligence, beauty, truth and goodness can be considered types of light, then an insight that stretches as far back as Plato is correct: Light is something very good and that goodness shines through in many forms.

We believe there came a time when light spoke, and the word it uttered was love in the form of a human being. And so it was that the man Jesus was called "the light that shone in the darkness" (see John 1:5).

Worship

We are all familiar with the many forms of worship taught to us from the time we were very young. The assumed place of worship is a church, a mosque or a temple. Services may last an hour or so. There is a sense of reverence, hymns, a homily, a collection and all the rest that goes into a bona fide religious service.

But we cannot worship God without serving one another. And we serve others through our daily work—both paid and unpaid.

Labor is truly human: washing clothes; writing a letter; preparing a meal; driving a bus; opening a door…letting the living revelation of God pass through our lives. That is real worship.

Straight and Crooked Nails

We all need to bend in different ways to make our lives go with the grain.

There are days when everything goes right and it is easy to stand tall and to feel glad to be alive. Such days can fill us with a kind of pride, when so much seems to come our way.

There are other days, however, when no matter how hard we try nothing seems to go right. And the harder we try the more frustrated we become. Most days, though, fall somewhere in the middle.

Those with whom we share our lives, be they our family, co-workers or significant others, experience life in much the same way. We all share the same plank. When we notice someone getting bent out of shape, we should lean a bit and offer some help. And if we need help, we should lean as best we can toward someone who wants to help us. We all need to bend in different ways to make our lives go with the grain.

Porch in the Sun

Come ye apart and rest a while.

89

When Silence Seems to Speak

Back in New Jersey, I would often see people in church, very early in the morning, as I got ready for Mass. There were usually not more than two or three, but as they prayed in the darkened church I could feel the soft language a quiet church speaks in the early hours.

I don't know if the people I saw were worrying about how they prayed or what they said. They seemed to be listening to the peace. And as they listened and as they prayed, their presence became my prayer.

They were scattered bits of light in the darkness of the morning. Their waiting and silence reminded me of the presence of God. But I never told them. Maybe I should have, but it didn't seem necessary. They would have been surprised to hear they said so much to me…without ever uttering a word.

Wine and Friends

Relationships with God abound with stories of feasts, friendships and intimacies of abiding human love. Many of the images Jesus used to describe the Kingdom were feasts. The "end time" is to be a time of joy. The breaking of the eternal into the finite will come as a celebratory feast. Some may ask why this can't happen right away. Some may wonder why, if God wants friendship, we aren't brought immediately into his fold.

Friendship takes time. Jesus enjoyed the company of men and women and he especially enjoyed sharing meals. He learned of friendship through sharing food and wine with all kinds of people.

There is something sacramental to every meal we share. A meal should be a sign of friendship, a symbolic ritual. God is present in the breaking of bread, the sharing of wine, the telling of stories. Our stories are those of God as well. As we grow and learn trust, fidelity, warmth and comfort through friends gathered around a table, we are learning how God takes our time and makes it sacred. It is a sign of a life yet to come, a life we already share.

Shed in Field

Scholars sometimes refer to world religions as "systems." Some religious systems are therefore said to be open to the world while others are more elitist or closed, although most religions carry variations of each.

Christianity can be likened to a three-walled shelter. It is open to the world, it affords a good view, and it offers comfort regardless of the weather. It can be a moveable shelter too—able to be brought to new places wherever there is a need for it.

All symbols of what it means to be Christian should be open: a home, a shelter, a church, a God.

Do Not Take

Life abounds in boundaries. There is not one species that does not conform to boundaries. Even non-organic forms of matter follow laws and certain restrictions. But we humans share this need for boundaries. Things can get ugly when we test the limits of human relationships. We experience jealousy, possessiveness, greed, hardness of heart: things that cannot let love in or out.

The love of God, however, is boundless and beyond measure. God's days are beyond counting; God's mercy is overflowing.

It is not yet time for us to share fully in God's life. But we have been promised that day will come. Until then, we need a lot of wisdom to know what it is that we have a right to keep, like our integrity, and no right to keep—those things in life that should be shared. No small part of wisdom is the discernment needed to come up with ways to better share who we are and what we have with the poor.

Gates

When life gets a bit out of control, it is common to hear people say they're "going through something," as if there is clarity on one side of the "something" and more clarity on the other. And yet it is true that we are always going through something, be it a day, a door or a conversation.

Everything that comes our way offers a passage from one way of being to another. It is not good to detour these passages—they invite us through to something or someone new.

Be open to what lies ahead. There are many who have already passed through whatever may come our way. And the wisest of us are looking over our shoulders, willing to offer encouragement to those behind us.

Dry Periods

We all know those times when, no matter what we do, we cannot force the inspiration needed to write a poem or compose a song or say a prayer. Passion between lovers ebbs while the warmth that should be shared gives way to a strange chill. Dry periods come and go. But maybe each of these has a purpose.

We do what we can to get the creativity flowing again.

The response to prolonged dry periods might be two-fold: Patience, for one, and the wisdom not to blame your spouse, friend, God…or the weather.

Solitude

I was at the airport one day and everywhere I looked people were using cell phones. Everywhere I went, people were talking animatedly on those small and convenient devices. On the way back to the monastery, I noticed drivers chatting away as they maneuvered their cars along the interstate. With great ease and one monthly payment, people were connecting with other people both near and far, twenty-four hours a day.

Looking at all those people connecting so easily wherever they went, it made me wonder if they missed solitude. Some people panic when they're cut off, for one reason or another, from the communication that modern technology affords.

We get used to being alone here at the monastery. Phones are not a significantpart of the monastic "loop." In some ways, this may seem like a big disconnect, but I don't feel that way. Humans need solitude. We need a way to get some distance from "it all." We need some space to better be at peace with ourselves and others. Everyone has a bit of the monk in them. We carry a little chip inside of us that is reserved for connecting with God—and there are times we need to find the buttons that make that chip glow.

Inspiration

We often overlook the ways the Spirit comes to us.

Placement of Light

Prayers go heavenward every day so that the Spirit might come and inspire us. The gifts of the Spirit are many. Wherever there is goodness, in all its manifestations, it is the work of the Spirit.

We often overlook the ways the Spirit comes to us. Perhaps we are waiting for one thing amidst all the other gifts. Or we want something right away but the Spirit works according to its own time and its own ways.

In the quiet of the morning, it is good to take a walk and listen with our steps. Walking slowly, we can imagine the day in its entirety as an infinite array of answered prayers.

Light exists. But light cannot be seen on its own. It can only be seen when there is something else to reflect it, as if light needs a place to rest in order to be revealed.

God is similar. We see only where God's effects take place and rest amid our lives.

Perhaps then, eternity is the gradual unfolding of all that God is—through all that God loves. If so, there will be more and more light, as love finds ways to settle and shine on every place, through everyone.

Heart of Matter

Matter may seem impenetrable. And the word "matter" covers a lot of ground—from the earth beneath our feet that turns hard without moisture to the human heart that turns hard without love.

But the presence of God is a living presence that transforms all of existence into a new way of being.

There is a song, "Love Is in the Air." That is truer than we know. Love is everywhere, moving all things to a lasting place in the heart of God.

What Shines Through

We do not see things as they really are. People and places, everything around us, comes to us through symbols. As in language or art, a photograph or a memory, we can only grasp what "is" through the medium of the symbolic.

We Christians believe that God came to us through a person, Jesus of Nazareth. And because of that person, we believe there is more to life than only what we see. God also comes to us through a vast array of people, experiences, memories and hopes; nothing is void of the presence of God.

The saints and mystics among us are many. Through how they live or what they say and create, they invite us to experience life a little differently. And the best among them invite us to trust the God who shines through everything about us, through all that is seemingly ordinary and commonplace.

Faith

The gift of faith helps us get from one place to another.
It gives us balance. We learn the finer arts of beauty.
It is something we can share. It offers great scenery and
lots of people along the way. It is also free—there are no
strings attached.

Should we fall along the way, others will help us.

Faith helps to slow us down, to move us along when we
need to reach great heights, so that when the day is done
we can rest and wake with hope again in the morning.

Light from Darkness

Not long ago I came across a phrase that really struck
me. It was in a letter from a friend of mine who found this
apparently anonymous line: "I love the darkest of nights,
because the stars shine all the more brightly."

It is common for people to fear the dark. They take little or
no comfort in the stars. They feel more at ease in the light
of day. But darkness is not only a vehicle for light—there
can be no light at all without darkness.

We believe that God will dispel all darkness, but until then
we grope our way through our days and nights. The stars
offer their far-away light to give us comfort—and some
delight—to ponder. And they shine well into the day.

Light Around Every Corner

There is always some light around every corner.

Bird and Cross

Much has been written about the meaning of life. There are those who find comfort in religion. There are more who rely on philosophy. And there are those who turn to science in an attempt to understand life's meaning and to control it.

Of course, there are as many ways to find meaning as there are people in the world. Our need to understand life's purpose is as necessary as the air we breathe.

We need something or someone to live for. It may be thematically undeveloped or spiritually vague, but if we find a meaningful life we can reach a height of human achievement that has nothing to do with material accomplishments or acquisitions. To find something or someone who ignites a loving passion in our hearts is to know the true meaning of life. We were meant to discover the beauty of living a life in service to others.

Ladder and Vine

Every step in the direction of good is growth.

Old Age

Our years have a way of creeping up on us. My grandmother used to say that her life seemed like a dream—it went by so fast.

Our society could do a lot better when it comes to revering age. Many good things come with the passing years: maturity, wisdom, patience, a mellow spirit. These and more are granted with the advanced degree called old age.

It is a beautiful sight to see a child cling to a grandparent. It is as if the child knows there is something important to be learned from one who is older and wiser. When we are young, we are open to all kinds of possibilities and have the energy to pursue them. In our later years, we find a need for stillness, for time to recollect and share our recollections with the young. The possibilities are many— all those stories we have to share!

Discerning Light

Priests of ancient times are known to have practiced rituals to keep the universe going. They believed the proper and faithful execution of ritual appeased the gods. They believed their prayers brought the sun to the horizon each morning.

We may be wiser in this modern age. We no longer pray to bring about the universe and all its wonders. We take the arrival of morning for granted. Whereas the sun may shine without any help from us, however, there is a darkness that can only be dispelled through a conscious movement of the human spirit.

The light that is wisdom born of love can only shine when we reach for it and learn from it. If every man and woman awoke each day to pray and hold fast to the light that is love, the world would be a place less darkened by the blackness of hatred, indifference, fear and prejudice.

Leaves on a Path

There is a non-profit foundation that encourages us to practice random acts of kindness.

It is a beautiful way to live. Any given day offers opportunities to "do the good that presents itself" as Saint Vincent de Paul once said. These need not be premeditated or planned out. Spontaneity is more the rule.

Such kind acts can fall from one's life into the paths of others and take root. Kindness has a way of growing.

Moving Toward the Light

Something of God shines through everything.
Look about and follow the light wherever you may find it.

There are creatures living in the deepest depths of the oceans that are capable of generating their own light in order to make their way through the darkness. Most living things need light to live. Plants grow toward light. We have trees here on our property where one side flourishes while the other withers because it lacks access to light.

Most of us take light for granted. It is a wondrous gift that enables us to see and to find our way through any given day.

Love is a reflection of the light that is God, and indeed our lives are a journey toward the fullness of love that is the eternal light of God.

We go through our days and there are dark times and painful times, times when the light seems far away. It is wise to learn from our fellow creatures with which we share life—creatures that move steadily or crane toward the light they need for sustenance. Something of God shines through everything. Look about and follow the light wherever you may find it.

Afternoon

How beautiful is the afternoon.

Banquet Hall

Some Spice and Growth

There is the parable Jesus told about the king who arranged a great feast but those whom he invited did not come. So he sent his messengers far and wide to invite others—and then the banquet hall was filled with people from the byroads of life.

The earth is the banquet hall of God. Everyone is invited to gather and to feast. Many tables are yet empty. The invitation stands—we need to make room at our table for the hurting and the stranger, the lonely and the downhearted. They have claim to the best seats. They have a right to the hope that a Christian way of life can give.

Just like a good cook's long preparation before a meal, God has given each of us the chance to take a gourmet approach to life. We have plenty to choose from in order to make our life something of a feast. With the right seasonings, a blend of proper time and temperatures, patience and risk, our life can be a delicacy.

Most importantly, our life can be a feast for others.

Brilliant Orange Trees

We hope for that special something or someone, and the hope can be so blinding that we miss what else is pouring out all around us.

Hope is a wondrous gift, but if it narrows our focus we can easily lose sight of all the goodness about us—things we never ask or hope for but that come our way each and every day.

Birdland

We need to get our own house in order before we take it upon ourselves to set about fixing the homes of others.

It is only human to blame those who don't quite see things our way. We call them short-sighted, we say they're missing the point or that they're out to lunch. Sometimes they just seem plain stupid. Why don't they appreciate our words of wisdom? Only with a large dose of humility can we see into our own house. It is much easier to ruminate about the sorry lives of others.

A spiritual home is like a person whose heart is an open house or one of those friendly, twenty-four-hour diners. A welcome sight along the road, always open, friendly and non-judgmental. An ideal spot for weary travelers.

Growth

Blogs are places online where people can post writings, photographs and links to other sites. Because the Internet has a world-wide reach, there are blogs from countries near and far. Many folks write very well about God, love, daily occurrences or political and social concerns. And there are many parents who post the day-to-day progress of their children—these blogs are primarily about growth.

Growth may have a lot to do with accepting our own limitations as well as the limitations of others. And growth is not solely an individual enterprise. Personal growth seems to have a lot to do with those around us. It seems to have a social dimension.

No matter how comfortable our upbringing, we yearn for something we can't provide for ourselves.

More Than a Fair Exchange

Codes of exchange, either quite up-front or discretely subtle, are the ways we negotiate everything from human relationships to the price of olives. The patterns may fluctuate, depending on many things, not the least of which is gleaning some kind of profit from the exchange. Which means of course that it is the rare exchange that is mutually fair. Life is a parade of winners and losers—or at least this is one way of looking at it.

But there is another way. Some things are given to us free, with no strings attached. Think of those who loved you and asked for nothing back. Or better yet, think of when you were in a position to be of real help to someone and felt the near delirious sensation of wanting nothing back. It is a freeing feeling, if only because we then know in our hearts that there really are exchanges in life that reflect something of how we really should live as brothers and sisters.

Redemption is usually understood as an exchange of something for an equal or even greater good. But churches enshrine a hope for a risk-free redemption. God is more than fair. If we find the capacity to love, life can be an ongoing bonanza of redemption.

Hope

If we hope for things eternal, we will begin to see things in life quite differently.
Eternity is, in large measure, a way of seeing.

Gift of the Ordinary

There is splendor in the commonplace. As years pass, the memory of the common good takes root in our hearts.

We should remember to behold the ordinary and treasure it as an index to the way God wants us to love. Everything then becomes a tabernacle revealing the God within.

Fence Flower

An artist has a disciplined eye that notices things not readily seen by a casual observer. The beauty of an object quite unworthy of note can be revealed by a delicate interplay of light, shadow, color and form.

The first Christians were known by the way they loved. They were also well-noted for the eye they had for beauty.

Beauty is another way God tells us something about divinity. The humblest things in life are beautiful if we take the time to see them. Some of the most beautiful people are simple people who see beauty everywhere, because God is in their hearts.

The Blues

We get depressed, out of sorts, in a funk, so we do what we can to cheer ourselves up. There are all sorts of remedies for lifting the blues. Some are good and some are not so good. But there are times when the blues won't lift and we have to live with them for a while.

Beautiful things can be born from the blues. Of course there is the music—the blues themselves—those sad, plaintive and heart-rending songs that may not dispel their source of inspiration but surely rise above it. And then there are those who write when feeling down—and their words lift the spirits of those who read them.

There is something redemptive when words born from sorrow touch a human heart. That is what we want to make of the blues in our lives. They are put there for a reason. They may not feel good, but still we trust the highs and lows of life and cling to the God who lives in both.

Something Small Makes a Difference

We stitch the tapstery with love, day by day.

Some of Us Grow Differently

The world is vast. Life seems long. Mountains tower. We cannot see the far side of an ocean nor can we see its depth.

Despite the immensity about us and within us, it seems that we were made to deal with it step by step, bit by bit. Even the most impressive plans require modest and finely-detailed moves. Nothing is accomplished by one great leap.

To value the micro is to learn to view life in all its wonderful particularities. A great life is like a beautiful tapestry woven over time. We stitch the tapestry with love, day by day, content not to finish it all at once.

When we were very young, we saw everything in terms of our needs. We couldn't help but think of ourselves first. A significant part of this selfishness was a very low tolerance for the differences we saw in other people. Early friendships were based on likeness; life was just easier that way. Anyone who was different was easily cast aside to the far side of the playground.

The scenario changes as we grow older. We gradually move into a world where differences are all over the place. Of course, we can choose to act immaturely and keep those who are different at bay. We can categorize people we do not understand or appreciate by putting them into potentially harmful slots, labeling them as being worthy of an "in" or "out" existence.

But God made us different for a reason. It is good for our hearts to appreciate the amazing differences that constitute human beings. We learn to be more loving when we become more open to the many faces of God.

Vine Fence Flowers Garden

A little beauty goes a long way.

Cloister Walk

It is often said that contemplation is a very refined and special activity of the mind, something that only monks and holy people do. Because there are places set apart for the refined search for God, it is assumed that those who reside there have some kind of an edge on the God-market.

But there is something of the monk in everyone.

We all know and cherish places where we can gather ourselves, our thoughts, our loves. And we monks know that what we strive for is to be found everywhere: airports, kitchens, diners and beaches…and cloister walks.

Stations of the Cross

*We see something on a road and stop to realize the meaning of life
is often hidden amidst the ordinary, asking only that we pause, look, ponder.*

Beauty and Speech

Beauty returns again and again. Creation abounds in beauty. Creation carries within itself the seeds of beauty and its return.

God made most beauty silent so that we could better appreciate the gift of language. But beauty has a lot to say to us. We listen to it all the time.

If beauty could speak to you, what would it say?

Other books by James Stephen Behrens, OCSO

GRACE IS EVERYWHERE: REFLECTIONS OF AN ASPIRING MONK

Take a look inside a Trappist monastery through the eyes of gifted priest and author James Stephen Behrens. Let his insightful, touching stories introduce you to the monks who live there and the lay people who come to enrich their lives. Marvel as he looks at ordinary events and realizes that God's grace is everywhere. Learn how monastic spirituality can impact your everyday life in a positive way.

ISBN: 0-87946-195-0
$12.95, paperback, 160 pages

"Behrens has crafted these essays as a kaleidoscope,
allowing us to observe through them different facets of the sacred in the ordinary.
His lens catches the stuff of life and holds it to the light of grace."
—From the Foreword by Dolores Leckey

MEMORIES OF GRACE: PORTRAITS FROM THE MONASTERY

Faithful followers and first-time readers alike will welcome this collection of vivid, colorful verbal portraits of people, places and events. James Stephen Behrens paints these memories of grace with the clarity, precision and warmth that brings each character and situation to life. He weaves the everyday and the unusual into the fabric of his portraits, always seeing and sharing the presence of God and the lingering memory of grace in each story.

ISBN: 0-87946-220-5
$12.95, paperback, 160 pages

"Behrens witnesses and pays tribute to the grace of God
eternally sacred and yet so commonplace."
—*America*